ABANDONED EAST TENNESSEE

RUINS OF ROCKY TOP

JAY FARRELL

AMERICA THROUGH TIME®
ADDING COLOR TO AMERICAN HISTORY

America Through Time is an imprint of Fonthill Media LLC
www.through-time.com
office@through-time.com

Published by Arcadia Publishing by arrangement with Fonthill Media LLC
For all general information, please contact Arcadia Publishing:
Telephone: 843-853-2070
Fax: 843-853-0044
E-mail: sales@arcadiapublishing.com
For customer service and orders:
Toll-Free 1-888-313-2665

www.arcadiapublishing.com

First published 2020

ISBN 978-1-63499-209-1

Typeset in Trade Gothic 10pt on 15pt
Printed and bound in England

CONTENTS

ABOUT THE AUTHOR

Jay Farrell is a Nashville, Tennessee, based photographer who loves photographing abandoned structures. He has a passion for utilizing his camera to share the unique, distressed beauty of abandoned homes and structures that most of the world has forgotten. Sharing his adventures with the public through authorship and blogging inspires him as much as the adventures themselves.

INTRODUCTION

The "life after people" feel to abandoned buildings—complete with rotted and caving floors, forgotten contents of yesteryear, and the overall entropy and distress—are what fuels my inspiration. There's a freedom (and a danger) of hitting the open road and exploring the backroad to seek these abandoned treasures. These structures tell a story. My goal while photographing these structures is to tell those stories and be their voice after they've been forgotten, sometimes for generations.

There is a process to my work. I don't force my way in or vandalize and I don't take or disturb anything. This shows a level of respect and reduces liability. These places are sometimes a hideout for squatters or vandals, which adds potential danger to the situation. It's extremely rare for me to be confronted by an heir or property owner, but it can happen. The structures are dangerous, with roofs caving in, broken glass, nails, needles, wildlife, loose boards, and weak floors. You must know what is under your feet—another reason I prefer to go with a trusted colleague if that option is available. It's eerie; there are lots of noises, creaks, and constant echoes.

This book features my travels and adventures in East Tennessee. Sure, East Tennessee is known for its beautiful Smoky Mountains, green meadows and rolling hills, curvy mountain roads, sunsets, wildflowers, rivers, streams, lakes, and overall quaint feel. You'll see none of that in this book. I will take you with me on a journey through some of the most dilapidated structures that most people only imagine—houses and storefronts that are surrounded by fallen materials and overgrowth, all suffering the effects of time.

It's not for the faint of heart, but the walls always tell stories and I enjoy the adventures. In this book, I will make my audience part of the adventure. I take you up close and personal to these tumbling structures, far deeper than the roadside view. You will experience the true feel of East Tennessee through my lens. I hope you enjoy it!

Take only pictures, leave only footprints. [*Illustration by Kelly J. King*]

1

HELLFIRE AND BRIMSTONE

I believe in happy accidents. It's funny how memory and thoughts work. Several years before this adventure, I drove through this little unincorporated town in Smith County, on the way to photograph a wedding. I remember seeing a roadside abandoned cafe with an old Mobil sign, but unfortunately, I didn't have time to stop. Somehow, I forgot all about it until this random day, years later, that I set out to find it. I knew it may not be there, but there was a chance it was, because developers aren't all over rural areas like they are in Nashville.

If it wasn't there, I'd explore backroads until I found an abandoned treasure of some sort. No harm, no foul. You could throw a rock from one end of the town to the other, so it didn't take long to cover it. All the sudden, I spotted an old abandoned church next to a graveyard, which quickly became my priority. I entered the property through a spring-loaded cemetery gate that made a subtle squeak when opening it.

Churches depend on member support to keep their doors open, pay the pastor's salary, and do community work. Sometimes, churches like this fold due to lack of attendance and financial support. Other times, the church gets in a state of disrepair, and it is no longer practical to maintain it. I'm just wondering if the slight fire damage had anything to do with its demise, or if that happened after the fact.

After leaving the church, I found the cafe that I was looking for to begin with. The building was not interesting or distressed, therefore not worth taking up prime real estate in this book. But the sign and the old kerosene/gas pump makes a nice bonus for this chapter. Finding something better than the reason I ventured there only proves that new adventures always wins over memory.

Still standing despite being partially burned by fire and choked by weeds.

Horror movies are made in places like this.

The inside of the old church was battered and bare.

These are some especially hideous fake flowers, but it's the thought that counts.

Step into my office.

This was most likely the pastor's quarters.

Above left: The rear view of the property that backed up to lots of brush and a creek.

Above right: Fire damaged siding.

A much more desolate view than in decades gone by, where I envision people in dress clothes gathering on Sundays.

Left: If only the building was in similar condition.

Below: A classic Mobil gas sign that you rarely see anymore. A worthy subject indeed.

2

GRAB A PLATE

On a misty, overcast, and chilly late October morning, I made the two-hour trek from Nashville to Belvidere, in Southeast Tennessee, to photograph a wedding by the falls. It was gorgeous, and a true portrait of East Tennessee beauty, with a wide variety of landscape. Here you can enjoy some of the nicest mountains, lakes, rivers, waterfalls, and farmland in the country. I've enjoyed river rafting, canoeing, mountain biking, and hiking there, and now abandoned building photography. I'm not quite brave enough for kayaking, at least on the Ocoee River, where I've gone whitewater rafting with my friends. There's a certain country charm and pride of "Rocky Top" amongst residents and UT football fans in East Tennessee.

On the road to Belvidere from Interstate 24, I saw nothing abandoned, but backroads are usually where the best ones are found. After the wedding, on the way back to Nashville, I decided to make a beeline and explore some roads less traveled. There were different two-lane blacktops to explore with twists, turns, and plenty of straightaways, all navigating me through the sparse Southeast Tennessee countryside. I knew I chose my roads well when I saw a brush-choked farmhouse sitting off the road. There was nowhere to pull off the road, but several hundred feet past the house was a church, so I borrowed their parking lot. There wasn't a soul or house around anywhere I could see.

That far out in the country, people recognize their sounds. All I could hear was the softly whistling wind and a few loud trucks racing by. Everything else was silent. When exploring abandoned houses, it's impossible to be completely quiet, because of all the debris under my feet that is impossible to avoid. I left no trace of my presence, and soon vanished into thin air, with only these photos that will remain.

Above: This farmland still appeared to be active, but the house was long forgotten. These two farm trucks under the utility barn roof may still be used.

Left: This told me two things. It was miles to the nearest gas station. Also, the farm was busy enough to need gas often.

The roadside view of the house. As you can see, my path inside was not easy. Per usual. But the goal was to get there fast and get out of plain sight.

Welcome home, sorry about the mess.

This recliner was in better shape than anything else in that house.

I don't think water and fertilizer are bringing this plant back to life.

Above: Nice view from the mud room into the kitchen. Watch your step.

Right: Not much freshening up is done in this bathroom anymore.

Left: This kitchen may be ransacked, but I bet there have been some delicious Sunday dinners cooked here, maybe a couple decades ago.

Below: Toaster, can opener, canned food, plates, petrified food remnants, all there.

They're old school, no dishwasher. The person behind the sink was the dishwasher.

One of the bedrooms that I couldn't walk far inside.

The smell of mold and mildew was especially bad in this bedroom with lots of wet contents.

Maybe wildlife lives in this living room now.

Above left: Grab a plate, serve yourself. Just wipe off the years of accumulated dirt and dust.

Above right: Land ho! This boat doesn't hold water too well if a tree can grow through it.

A utility barn behind the house, through very thick brush.

3

THE ABANDONED OASIS

Abandoned building exploring may be a rather unconventional way to spend Christmas day, but I never claimed to be normal. Many people have this holiday image of happy families sitting around a fire drinking hot cider, but I think I've found peace with being a misfit of sorts. I just wanted to experience the freedom of the backroads of East Tennessee instead of dealing with social situations that day.

One of my friends and readers, Julie, accompanied me on this Christmas outing, as she is fascinated with the blight of the abandoned. A full fuel tank and coolers packed with water and sandwiches would send us on our journey. The first random destination was Bledsoe County, South of Cookeville. After leaving city limits and the four-lane highway, approximately a half-mile after turning down the first random backroad, I saw this beautiful, abandoned, Victorian-era farmhouse. Because we were on the road for nearly two hours by then, and this was the first backroad we explored, I wondered if this was a mirage, or if I just had amazing beginner's luck.

It's not uncommon to find abandoned houses on active farmland, even houses with this level of character. One might ask, why would someone let this gorgeous house just sit there and fall apart? Here are my theories. Perhaps a family member or previous generation lived in the house and passed on, and over the years, the disrepair of the house kept getting worse. Maybe it stays up because of sentimental reasons. Other times, heirs haven't done anything with it. The cost of renovation or demolition is likely a factor, particularly in areas where industry has declined, causing economic downfall in the community. As long as the house isn't eating any hay in the meantime, they're no worse off. Some abandoned houses have obviously been used for junk storage, but that doesn't appear to be the case with this one. This was a high quality find, and I only hoped this would be a harbinger of what was to come on this day's outing.

I still couldn't believe my eyes at just how incredible and rare a stop this was. I told Julie we should work our way around back to get out of view and photograph those angles along the way. The next step was checking for inside access.

The side of the house. It only kept getting more interesting.

A linear shaped addition on the house perhaps. The kitchen was separate from the living quarters. This was common for homes from that era.

The only doorway in this utility barn, and a very low one, tells me this may have been a smokehouse. Envision the succulent smell and taste of the home cooked meats likely from their own farm-raised bovine and hogs.

Right: Admiring the stone foundation and blocks gathering moss.

Below: By now, my heart was pumping, so excited to get inside. I just had to very carefully navigate across the rotten deck boards. I looked for the nail holes to find floor joists, which weren't very solid either.

1950s-era range and sink cabinet (possibly older) was all that remained in this kitchen. Wood paneling and window frames told me this section was added onto the original house.

This would make a perfect horror movie setting if blood were splattered on the walls and floors. It's creepy on its own, nonetheless.

Above left: Handmade shelving in a utility room.

Above right: Someone may have used this old exercise bike while watching Richard Simmons on the old Admiral TV you're about to see.

Antique upright piano and filing cabinets in a neighboring room from the kitchen.

Above: The living room in the main part of the house, cluttered with miscellaneous debris.

Left: Of course I couldn't resist going upstairs, and the staircase was very solid.

Attic room with a gutted mattress, which means one thing: it's very old.

Interesting combination of a 1960s Admiral TV and a specimen jar with a dead snake. This would really creep out the average bear, and I must admit, it got my attention, too.

Someone never finished the plaster work or painting, with the seventy-eight cans of paint sitting in the corners.

The view from the upstairs window.

Remarkable character, texture, and color of the plaster and old wood floors.

Wait, there's more paint? All of it is probably dried up by now.

The back part of the attic room, with dramatic shadow play and layers of dirt and debris.

The other front angle of the grand home, once proudly lived in.

4

WATCH YOUR STEP

We were in for as authentic of an experience as one could get, turning on this one particular Bledsoe County backroad. It was full of twists and turns, going straight up the mountain, with sudden drop-offs. On top of that, the road narrowed the farther we drove up the mountain. There were very few residences, and I got the feeling that locals know when strangers approach. On the descent back down the mountain road, I was thinking, "This would not be the place to experience brake problems." This is where you quickly learn the value of downshifting. Once we reached the foot of the mountain, a burly, bearded mountain man in a pickup truck saw us coming and was nice to pull off so we could get by. I waved as a way to tell him thank you. He waved back, but I could tell he knew we weren't from there by the somewhat untrusting look he had on his face.

After a couple hours of backroad exploring and coming up empty, I approached Rhea County to see what abandoned treasures were in store for us. There were several that I passed by that weren't quite interesting enough. Although the mountain roads and overlooks were fun, I remembered the reason for the mission. By far the best road we discovered in the Rhea County leg of the journey declined into a valley, there sat a dilapidated house sitting farther from the road. It was a bit difficult to see from the road, even though the overgrowth was dormant for the winter, but still thick.

Approaching the front porch, Julie heard me utter some choice expletives when I stepped on a board with a rusty nail as it went through my shoe. The soles were fairly stiff and getting this board out wasn't easy. Julie saw me yank it out—she was either too passive aggressive or squeamish to assist. I jest. Thankfully I had a tetanus shot earlier that year!

I told you it wasn't easy to see. It looked fairly ordinary from the outside, but soon you'll see why this made the book.

This was right before I stepped on the nail—that sucked. Oh well, it could have been worse. The show must go on, as it did.

There was no access from the front door, so this meant getting attacked by briers and prickly brush to access the side entrance. The lounge chair and toilet were quite welcoming.

The back bedroom was a furniture dump, for 1960s or maybe 70s-era furniture.

Someone scavenged the tub and toilet tank. Either way, I love the creepiness of this bathroom.

The conversation pit. Julie decided not to enter, as the floors were bad. I took the chance. I did verify there was no basement level beneath.

The other bedroom served as a squatter shelter at some point.

After some research, I learned that these old Temco gas heaters were made here in Nashville.

It never fails. At least the soft, dreamy light peeking through the window made this gutted box spring/mattress look a smidgen more inviting. Or maybe not.

This old Coolerator electric stove was a rare find and a highlight of this house. I had never heard of the brand until then. It was in operation from 1908 to 1954. The company manufactured electric stoves, refrigerators, freezers, and air conditioners.

Above: On the way out, I had to document this lovely green lounge chair. The algae colored furniture collection brought to you by yours truly. You're welcome.

Right: I think the house is growing a beard. I was just happy I didn't fall through the floor, on top of stepping on a rusty nail and having to treat a puncture wound for a week.

5

SORRY, WE'RE CLOSED

Because we were far from any interstates, I opted to take a different way back home, passing through Chattanooga before taking I-24 back to Nashville. I explored a few backroads off the two-lane highway along the way, but came up empty. I was curious about Marion County, so the plan was to navigate some backroads there to end the day, then head home. Through more windy, hilly mountain roads, I saw mostly open land, developed waterfront communities, and very little abandoned property. By that point, I was enjoying the scenery along Nickajack Lake and the Tennessee River, with the daylight we had left.

Before turning down another road that brought us back to the interstate to go home, I saw a nice remnant of true Americana: an old storefront, very reminiscent of a classic Tennessee lakeside market. When they were open, moons ago, they probably sold fishing gear, live bait, groceries, cold Cokes, beer, and maybe even gas for boats. I thought it was a unique and interesting find worthy of a quick stop.

As our adventure for that day was closing, my initial recap of the day lent itself to a feeling of disappointment, as being one of the least productive abandoned excursions I've gone on. When taking into account the time and miles traveled, with a lot of dead ends, it seemingly came up short. Some trips are better than others, and that's just the nature of the game. When I had time to reflect on the day and consider the great abandoned treasures I did find (especially the farmhouse!), and the adventure of exploring somewhere new, I had a different perspective. It's more about the hunt than the destination. I also felt reaffirmed that even when findings were slim, I kept my standards and only stopped for the best. It's important to know when to say, "Tomorrow's another day."

I can almost hear the loud pickup trucks pulling in, with their tires crunching over the gravel lot, and the sound of them racing down the road when exiting, perhaps for an early morning coffee and breakfast biscuit stop, or some fishing bait before a day on the lake.

Ice machine under repair, check back tomorrow. Or maybe the tomorrow after that. Just don't hold your breath.

This very old Coke machine was designed for the long neck glass bottles. If you look closely, you can see a built-in bottle opener under the drink selection buttons.

6

DEVILISHLY UNIQUE EXPERIENCE

I felt so inspired by the landscape and feel of East Tennessee from past adventures, I decided to do an impromptu two-day trip for more exploration. It was unseasonably warm for the middle of winter, with slightly misty conditions. With a cooler packed and the fuel tank full, it was time to set out early in the morning to begin my next journey out east. By the time I made it to the Cumberland Plateau, it had become very foggy and misty. It was a sinister, but scenic, part of the overall mood. I exited around Rockwood and Harriman, in Roane County, and started exploring some backroads there. After nearly two hours on the Interstate, I was eager to stretch my legs and switch to backroads where I could actively explore. Subsequently, I could build inspiration while taking in the mood of the mountains, countryside, and misty fog, all unique to the East Tennessee region.

This particular adventure didn't start off without a slight hitch. In the middle of nowhere, on a less traveled road, what were the chances of seeing a Roane County Sheriff appear as I hiked up the hill to access this old forgotten farmhouse? In my experience, it's almost unheard of. I had my camera around my neck as he slowed down to approach me. After a brief exchange of pleasantries, the officer confirmed that I was there to take photos. He asked if I knew the property owners, which I didn't. I introduced myself and told him about my books and how much I enjoy these adventures. By then, I think I established a trust factor, and fortunately, he found what I do interesting.

He told me not to go inside if it was posted (it was posted in the front, not the back), and to carefully enjoy. Because I wasn't acting nervous and was honest with the officer, he was receptive. I even told him I was continuing my East Tennessee exploration afterwards. I hiked up the hill through the brush and prickly bushes, as usual. I somehow knew this place wouldn't disappoint.

This was the initial view I saw from the road, a bit blocked by overgrowth.

The siding on the far side of the house and distressed pattern makes one complete work of art.

View from under the front porch. I love the funky green color!

A well-seasoned utility barn out back.

Left: Do I call this a garden shed or utility barn? Either way, I like it.

Below: The back view of the house. What did I see? An open back door, with no posted sign. Decisions, decisions. I know the sheriff gave me that precaution, but he must understand that you can't put cake in front of a kid without it being devoured.

Immediately greeted by Satan art, how welcoming. By now, this doesn't faze me.

What an adorable kitchen with neat retro colors.

The ransacked living room. I wonder why they blocked off the fireplace.

A mattress in the midstream stage of deterioration. This is the result of years of neglect, the elements, temperature, and humidity.

Okay Satanic graffiti artist, you made your point. I didn't see him upstairs either.

Maybe this is what the sheriff wanted to make sure I wasn't doing. Clearly there has been some squatter/drifter activity here.

Above left: Hallway strewn with literature.

Above right: The back porch, where we gather on the couch, watch TV, and do whatever else we do.

A family cemetery behind the house on the property.

Another small barn that wasn't faring too well.

7

THE WIND TUNNEL

I made my way to Sevier County to continue my exploration. One part of the area is more rural, and the other puts you closer to Gatlinburg and Pigeon Forge, which I was trying to avoid because it's more of a tourist attraction. My friend, David, who lives out that way, told me about a beautiful and very old farmhouse in the vicinity that has been sitting vacant for many years. It only made sense to investigate, because that was one of the areas on my radar for this trip.

It seemed like an unlikely place for such a magnificent old farmhouse. Despite the open land surrounding the house, it was located on a very busy two-lane highway, very close to the road. In an overgrown pull-off from the road, I took in the sights of this early 1900s-era farmhouse. One peculiar thing I noticed right away was there wasn't a window in the house. I photographed that angle of the house, which was perfect timing, because the sun peaked out from behind the house, giving a different feel, before cloud cover came back. I love a cloudy day for abandoned missions, as it completes the dark, sinister mood. Other times, I use the sun to my advantage. I could see there was no issue getting inside, but did so quickly to not attract attention.

This old house was an interesting find, and a testament to how well-built houses were in that era. Few contents remained, and I had to use what clues were left behind. The house itself told a rich story. Despite being solo, I had company as the wind passed through the house with no windows to stop it. White noise from cars and trucks passing by on the highway and tin roofing slapping in the wind also added to the atmosphere of the once-proud home.

Above: The highway view of this lonely shell of a historic home.

Right: The front porch was surprisingly solid. Even though it appears this house has been abandoned for decades.

Left: At least Southern hospitality still exists. They offered me a chair to relax and stay a while.

Below: The first sitting room to my left of the front entrance.

Right: A door with so much character and patina, I'm surprised it hasn't been scavenged. The windows may have been. Why else would they be missing?

Below: One of the downstairs rooms with an ugly chair. Look closely at the detail in the deck spindles laying on the floor.

One of four fireplaces sharing two chimneys.

Dimensions and depth in photography is a fun challenge and concept.

It's interesting what people used to use as wall covering, like this very old box.

This very old water heater was on the floor of the kitchen. No sink or cabinets remained.

I liked the color choice and peeling lead paint.

The busted glass windows above the front door, giving a vantage point of the front porch roof. These were the only windows left in the house at all.

Right: This staircase wasn't the most brilliant one I've seen, detail and style wise, but it was very solid, as was the flooring.

Below: The view from the staircase window. The house shows its age and distress, but is still hanging on.

One of the upstairs rooms with many layers of wall covering.

A bird's eye view from the top of the staircase. Even the upstairs floors were solid. The ceilings were high, making the fall that much farther.

Now that I had been inside, I could take my time admiring the outside.

The back of the house, overlooking many acres of open land.

8

THE ROAD TO NEWPORT

Usually, deciding which roads to explore is a random choice and spur-of-the-moment decision. I suppose developing a certain science makes certain navigation an educated guess. Other times, like the last farmhouse, someone trusted and respected my work enough to steer me in its direction (which is a true honor). I've experienced many different journeys, all with different outcomes. Sometimes I hit the jackpot with a moderate amount of exploring. Other times, I do longer periods of exploring, and have to be happy with less. In certain, and more rare, circumstances, I know the vicinity I am traveling to, because of good old-fashioned detective work. One thing all my adventures have in common is that both the journey and the destination make up the story of each.

I will take you along with me on my afternoon journey, navigating the backroads and two-lane highways of Sevier County, and Jefferson County/Dandridge, with Newport, Cocke County being the final destination for the day. The first destination I stopped at was an old storefront of some sort. It was a mere few feet from the road, which wasn't a particularly busy stretch. This was the genuine East Tennessee backroad experience: mountains, valleys, streams, rivers, houses with chickens in the front yard, and couches on the front porch. Their turf and way of life, with me documenting the highlights, makes for a good day. As I explored the outside of the building, curious chickens from the house across the road came close to investigate the stranger lurking.

The building was supported by the riverbank and had to be built accordingly. It is clearly now part of the forgotten past.

It was choked in overgrowth on the outside, and thankfully there was an open door for me to document the inside.

Some random furnishings, with the most random discovery to come.

Two very old chairs, from the 1950s or 1960s.

Some random debris in the back room. I had to watch for weak flooring due to the decline of the land.

I'm wondering what the story was with the hay bales in the corner. Maybe they were for the chickens.

An old bias ply tire and a bunch of crap. I call it photogenic.

A very short distance down the road, I saw two classic cars sitting in the woods, completely surrounded by brush, with their tires sinking into the ground. There are probably plenty of classic and antique car enthusiasts/restorers who search the countryside for hidden gems to try to buy and restore.

Above: According to my research, this is a 1973 Chevrolet Impala. It had a 400 emblem on the side of the car, revealing its original engine size.

Below: When researching the year of this Impala, I couldn't tell whether it was a 1960 or 1961, as the grille was hidden partially by fallen trees and brush.

The inside of the car, which I could view through the back window.

It was a 1960, because it had more prevalent bat wings in the back than the 1961 model.

On the way back to the highway, there was another very old house, probably from a similar era as the house in the previous chapter. The land was for sale, and it stood alone in an area that was growing. I'm afraid once a buyer comes along, it will be commercial property and this house will be razed. Unfortunately, all the windows were boarded up, making it super dark inside.

On the road to Newport, I made a quick stop at a picker's store that sold all kinds of antiques, old furnishings, and other collector memorabilia. It was an interesting chat with the shopkeeper learning about his business and the things he runs across. I also gave some attention to his longhaired Dachshund pup. Our stories were similar as far as things we see on our different types of adventures. It was a nice way to break up the trip and get a local experience.

This old gem sits on land that was likely a farm at one time.

Beautiful stone pillars and other cozy features would have made this a welcome home sight at one time.

Above left: Two antique porch chairs that many old timers probably enjoyed over the years.

Above right: The back breezeway.

9

THE DRIVE-IN THEATER

I arrived in Newport where I settled for the evening after a long day of navigating and exploring. I saw a sign that said "Drive-In" off to the side of the road, with part of it covered up. I thought it looked like an old drive-in movie theater. I decided to investigate, and sure enough—I saw a giant screen back from the road, buried in acres of brush. I've never spotted an abandoned drive-in theater before this, so I was eager to brave the vegetation and see what remained after decades of abandonment. That wasn't an easy accomplishment, but in I went. This was too rare of a find not to conquer the obstacles.

The speakers and poles where each car would park were gone. The possibility exists that an FM radio station was designated for patrons to listen in their cars or trucks. As I was walking across the old lot where moviegoers sat, there was a marshy, coarse grass under my feet, with thick brush and full-grown trees everywhere. Time completely took over. At one point, I was startled when I heard voices over a P.A. system, but then I remembered there was a car dealership across the street, with one department paging another.

Upon doing some research, I learned that the drive-in theater opened in 1965, and closed in 1998. At the time of my adventure, there was twenty years of overgrowth built up. I also learned that the projector was sold to a different drive-in theater in Watertown, TN. The projector booth and concession stand were razed, which is why I couldn't find them. I immediately thought of scenes from the movie, *American Graffiti*, with the Detroit steel of yesteryear and high school sweethearts on a Saturday night date, sharing popcorn and a Coke. This was a real American treasure that I was excited to close the day with.

The old ticket booth at the entrance.

I couldn't even guess what those used to be. But I love the retro blue color.

Above left: The fence that stopped freeloading onlookers from watching the show without a ticket.

Above right: The electrical panel for the screen. Now the trick was getting to the screen.

This was the clearest angle I could get of the screen.

The inside of another building, perhaps another ticket booth.

It had to be another ticket booth, as it was too small to be much else. With only one, the lines would be out past the road on a busy night.

The defunct entrance to the theater, which is sad to see as these drive-ins are an endangered breed.

Adjacent to the old screen was a small motorcycle shop. They semi-repurposed the sign, but thankfully left the nostalgia of the old drive-in sign.

10

HILLS AND HOLLOWS OF COCKE COUNTY

I've never been a morning person, but I was ready to get back to exploring soon after daybreak, after a halfway decent night's sleep. I thanked my hosts and went on my way to explore the desolate backroads of Cocke County. It was a cloudy and misty morning (which is very reminiscent of the Smoky Mountains), but visibility was clear. Soon into my journey, I knew this was as real of a backwoods East Tennessee experience as I could get. Certain houses that look abandoned may not be. That was the case in this area, and is always something to be mindful of.

First, I navigated my way through the most desolate backroads I could find in the Cosby area. The hills, hollows, hairpin turns, mountain mist, streams, and rivers all made up the ambience. I even spotted locals sitting on the porch of a local general store waiting for passing cars to wave to. Follow along the journey with the photos and captions, as there were quite a few quick stops along the way.

When I exhausted my resources there, I drove back through Newport to get to the other side of Cocke County, to an unincorporated town called Del Rio. My friend, Eric, grew up in this area, and assured me I'd find some treasures around there. He was definitely right. I found an abandoned storefront as I was exiting town. Then, after leaving town towards Del Rio, I spotted an abandoned store and gas station that caught my attention. Everything on that road backed up to the French Broad River, which was quite high from large volumes of recent rain.

The experience and perspective I want to provide is taking you up close and personal with the real East Tennessee backwoods hills and hollows—a deeper, more desolate vantage point through the eyes of an explorer of entropy, far beyond the adventures of the average mainstream tourist. Locals only see most of what I'm showing you in this book. That's why I avoid busier tourist areas, and venture off the beaten path.

I spotted a barn with an antique car sitting inside it and saw many car parts laying across the ground.

This is another find that car enthusiasts would only dream about or read about, unless they explore the remote corners of the earth. Remember what I was saying about a house looking abandoned when it really isn't? I believe the house further back on the property behind the barn may have been an example of this. This was my target destination here.

I have no doubt this house was abandoned, but sadly, there was no way in. Oh well. It was worth a stop.

The locked electric meter was the giveaway, and that it was indeed vacant.

Surrounded by mountainside and farmland sat an old abandoned general store.

Open whenever on all other days, but closed Sunday. This was a Tuesday, and they still weren't open. What gives? We might be waiting a while.

If there's any one photo I took this whole trip that belongs on a postcard, this is it.

A closeup of the small creek-side cottage.

There were layers of wall covering and gutted furniture, and not much else, left behind.

A compromised floor and extensive bottle collection.

Above left: The debris has likely sat there for decades.

Above right: I wonder if that door ever had a lock on it.

The sun came out to play for a moment. It was a nice halo for the utility barn on Rocky Top.

This was an abandoned storefront in Newport. It was pie shaped and built around the steep riverbank. It was a unique structure.

An old-time gas pump island, with a bright light. This was rather primitive. There was no rain shelter on this one.

Closed indefinitely, awaiting building repair and tree removal.

The hasp and lock on the front door wasn't fastened, so in I went. The warning sign on the door only addressed removal of property, and it said nothing about authors and urban explorers keeping out. I've never felt so welcome.

Shelving and a display case that has been used and abused.

Above left: The store dabbled in auto parts as well. But I saw no evidence of a past mechanic shop there.

Above right: I believe this is a very old Sprite sign.

The old Del Rio post office. A newer one has taken its place across the railroad tracks.

This rustic cabin would make a dream getaway or retirement cottage, complete with mountains for hiking and a babbling brook beside it. Someone left it to fall apart.

11

THE LOCAL EXPERIENCE

In the final leg of my journey, I traveled East Tennessee's most desolate backroads—roads where locals seldom see anyone they don't know. On a narrow, windy backroad nestled in the hills of Cocke County, buried in dormant shrubbery sat two abandoned houses deep in the woods. At the next house over, I saw an older gentleman sitting on his front porch. I knew that I would have to approach him to get access to those two forgotten backwoods treasures., despite that being unusual for me.

As I discreetly stopped, I expressed interest in photographing the abandoned houses in the woods, I asked if he knew their history, and if he would allow me to access the woods through his property. After exchanging pleasantries, he seemed eager for the visit, and introduced himself as Jimmy.

Jimmy told me that he had lived at this house for twenty-three years, and the houses were abandoned even then. Neighbors told him that the former resident left and never came back. I was even more excited to see what the houses had in store. I noticed a quaint rustic woodworking shop next to his house, which he eagerly gave me a tour of. Jimmy uses only hand tools, no power tools. He also showed me the ornate details in the door he made, with carvings similar to what I've seen in very old Victorian-era houses. In addition, he showed me how he draws these patterns, and the drawings hanging up in his workshop. It was cozy, complete with a wood stove. As I admired his skill, I heard the babbling brook in the background. Thankfully, Jimmy had rubber boots for me to borrow to get across.

Jimmy and I talked a few more moments before I went on my way. He was looking forward to enjoying some dinner and working on a new drawing that evening. Ironically, we both needed the visit and felt inspired because of it. I signed and handed him a copy of an earlier *Abandoned Tennessee* volume, and his eyes lit up. Now he is part of the story of *Abandoned East Tennessee*.

This may have been a small mother-in-law quarter or separate apartment. Nothing was inside it, but it was quite interesting given the backwoods location.

There were no signs of a driveway or roadway. There had to have been a bridge at one time over the creek.

Above left: The front porch caved in on the main house.

Above right: The front view of the main house, completely surrounded by trees and brush.

I knew there was no way inside from the front, as the porch was too rotted and too far of a drop. I was determined.

Above left: No more rocking chairs and sweet tea/moonshine sipping on this front porch.

Above right: I went around back, and saw moss growing on the tin roof.

A very old rusted water heater laying on the ground.

The floor was bad, but closer to the ground. My meal ticket.

Some very old jars and bottles.

No, that was not a Dutch angle, the sink cabinet really was that off kilter.

Appliances and furniture, complete destruction!

Rusted refrigerator, retro Thermos, and a whole host of other debris.

If the floor couldn't hold the couch any longer, I wasn't going farther in that room.

Above: I never recall seeing metal kitchen cabinets before, except sink cabinets. After approximately thirty years of abandonment, rust happens. It's not the only thing there that has suffered the effects of time. But that's good for me!

Left: A very old Frigidaire, 1960s-era, according to a knowledgeable source.

MORE BY JAY FARRELL

ABANDONED ALABAMA

ISBN: 978-1-63499-114-8

ABANDONED KENTUCKY
VOLUME 1

ISBN: 978-1-63499-056-1

ABANDONED KENTUCKY
VOLUME 2

ISBN: 978-1-63499-169-8

MORE BY JAY FARRELL

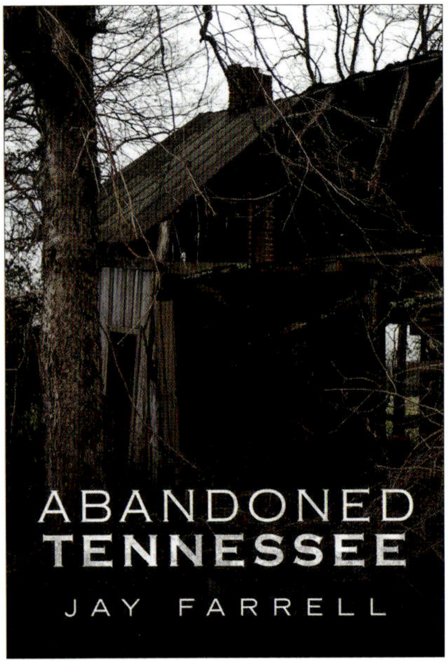

ABANDONED TENNESSEE
VOLUME 1
ISBN: 978-1-63499-055-4

ABANDONED TENNESSEE
VOLUME 2
ISBN: 978-1-63499-102-5

ABANDONED NASHVILLE
ISBN: 978-1-63499-113-1

ABANDONED MISSISSIPPI
ISBN 978-1-63499-179-7